Remembering When

*A Collection of Poetry
by
Jeffrey A. Angus
Rick Ducayne
Gabrielle R. West*

The NorGus Press Poetry Series
Volume Three

NorGus Press
Auburn, New York

Copyright © 2014 by NorGus Press

All stories contained in this volume have been published with permission from the authors.

All Right Reserved

No portion of this publication may be reproduced, stored in any electronic system, or transmitted in form or by any means, electronic, mechanical, photocopy, recording or otherwise, without written permission from the authors. This is a work of fiction. Any resemblance to any actual person, living, dead or undead, events, or locales is entirely coincidental.

ISBN-10: 1500698482

ISBN-13: 978-1500698485

Printed in the USA by NorGus Press

Front Cover Photo ~ "Tracks"
© Christopher Molloy

Table of Contents

Introduction ix

Remembering When 1
   by Jeffrey A. Angus

Smiley 2
   by Rick Ducayne

Call on me 4
   by Gabrielle R. West

Welcome Spring 6
   by Jeffrey A. Angus

Expiration Date 8
   by Rick Ducayne

Nature's Tantrum 10
   by Jeffrey A. Angus

Seek 12
   by Rick Ducayne

Is it time? 14
   by Jeffrey A. Angus

Close Shave 16
   by Rick Ducayne

I break for sunshine 18
   by Jeffrey A. Angus

Morning Altar 19
   by Rick Ducayne

The day is long but our time is short 22
   by Jeffrey A. Angus

Sweeper 24
   by Rick Ducayne

Ode to the phone 26
   by Jeffrey A. Angus

Slammer 28
   by Rick Ducayne

Feeling the Story 30
   by Gabrielle R. West

Life's Blacksmith 31
   by Jeffrey A. Angus

You Devil 32
   by Rick Ducayne

Fresh Air 34
   by Jeffrey A. Angus

The veil 35
   by Rick Ducayne

Life Poem 36
   by Jeffrey A. Angus

Duck! 38
   by Rick Ducayne

Mind's Eye 40
 by Jeffrey A. Angus
Don't Cram 41
 by Rick Ducayne
Tides of Service 42
 by Jeffrey A. Angus
Temperate Tempers 43
 by Jeffrey A. Angus
It's Not Over 44
 by Rick Ducayne
The Crucifix 46
 by Rick Ducayne
Colors of Life 49
 by Jeffrey A. Angus
Ug-oh 50
 by Rick Ducayne
Welcome to the family 53
 by Jeffrey A. Angus
Who's Crazy 54
 by Rick Ducayne
I Fear I Will Never Know 56
 by Jeffrey A. Angus
He Sees Him 58
 by Rick Ducayne

I fly through portals 61
    by Gabrielle R. West

Time is on my side? 62
    by Jeffrey A. Angus

Sparky 64
    by Rick Ducayne

Open Life 66
    by Jeffrey A. Angus

Dusty 67
    by Rick Ducayne

A flash of life 70
    by Jeffrey A. Angus

Thirsty 71
    by Rick Ducayne

Lunchtime 72
    by Rick Ducayne

Donor 74
    by Jeffrey A. Angus

Brave 75
    by Gabrielle R. West

Thinking of Melvin 76
    by Rick Ducayne

Tell me 81
    by Rick Ducayne

Remember The Day 82
   by Jeffrey A. Angus
Shoppers 83
   by Rick Ducayne
Slappy 84
   by Rick Ducayne
Normal Life Alone 86
   by Jeffrey A. Angus
Buckle up 88
   by Rick Ducayne
My Own Score Keeper 90
   by Jeffrey A. Angus
Not a Word 92
   by Rick Ducayne
We Aquarius 94
   by Gabriel West
Poet's View 95
   by Jeffrey A. Angus
Quiet Love 96
   A Short Story by Rick Ducayne
The Searching Self 110
   A Short Story by Rick Ducayne

About the Authors 130

Introduction

Norgus Press is always looking to introduce its readers to new writers. In this edition of the Norgus Press Poetry Series, we are proud to show you some work from a young poet who expresses her feelings in prose, giving us a glimpse of a teenager's view of the world around her. Please welcome Gabrielle R. West to the Norgus Press family. I hope you enjoy the poems in this volume and, as always, thank you for your support.

Jeffrey A. Angus

Remembering When
by Jeffrey A. Angus

Clouds snow white; I lie in the soft grass
The sounds of the birds and bees; relax and enjoy
The hot sun bakes; a comfort to my skin
I shade my eyes; a silver man-made bird flies high near the clouds
As it disappears I wonder…where is it going?

Thinking of times; past, present and future
The tension and anxiety from the day; lost in another world

Smiley
(Inspired by Psalm 8)
by Rick Ducayne

I once went through a period
of time when I was given
an
extraordinary
appreciation for the power and majesty
of God expressed in all
creation.
driving home from work
I would offer God praise, worship, thanks
and
adoration for everything that flashed by my
windshield.
every blade of grass
    every cloud in the sky
  the sky itself
the very idea of a sky
every individual tree and branch and leaf
each insect
the setting sun
   the sunset colors
all colors
the idea of colors and the joy each brings,
for the senses I possessed to take in these things
and the mind that He gave me which sang out in
   the car

of a return to God of that unimaginable love
which He showered on me by creating all this
   wonderment
and I reflected on all the detail, landscape, beauty
   and
breathtaking splendor in all the lands in
every corner of the earth
and even out into the seemingly endless universe
all just for my enjoyment.
my heart was exploding with love for my Creator
   Who
took sheer delight in giving me all the pleasures
of His creation.
I couldn't stop smiling during the entire one hour
   commute.
my face would actually start to hurt.
when I would get home it was all I could do to tone
   it down so
my family wouldn't think I had gone
mad.

it only lasted for a few days,
but
man,
it was really

something.

Call on me
by Gabrielle R. West

I am darkness, but let God's light show me the way.
Break me from this insanity.
Bring me to reality.

I am a shadow.
I cast myself upon the mortals I see.
Protecting them from danger, and out of God's way.

I am all her regrets.
I am her hate.
I am her anger.

She will stand above me.
Viewing my deceased body.
I should, I will, remain on this earth.

Let me stay with you
Let me be with you
Let me be your puppet.

Do you hear the whispers?
Voices of the Angel's?
They call for me.

NorGus Press

My body will be covered with soil
Deep down in the ground
And my soul will be free.

Welcome Spring
by Jeffrey A. Angus

The sun glares, the snow white, a blanket of cold covers the mountain side
Rocks jut out like fingers trying to claw their way through a drift
Footprints can be seen winding past the appendages.
An eagle screams as he passes over head, the echo to be sent across the valley.

Who is the artist that paints the canvas, Mother Nature?
She has washed the highest peaks with white, brown, green and gray.
The valley chasing away the blanket of ice and you can almost see it retreat up the side of the mountain
Early blooms of flowers in the meadow, a smile from the fox as it jumps through the grass.

Winter is leaving and the spring brings new life.
A cycle that makes the long winter month's tolerable.
The stream rides past, full of life and debris.
A deer takes a long drink and stands proud and resistant.

Thank you sunshine for giving this earth a chance
    to be reborn.
Welcome to the spring, growth and renew the spirit
    of life.
The warmth on our skin, detox the winter blues
Temperatures rise, do your magic and release
    hibernation

Welcome home my old friend, clouds so white.
All the residents' enjoy the freshness of the air.
Breathe deep as the sent only carries this time of
    year.
Walk into your lifespan and continue down the
    path.

Remembering When

Expiration Date
by Rick Ducayne

Books are like women:
some of them
have wonderful cover jackets with
    brilliant colors and
    lively reviews
but when you open them up
   you discover vapid emptiness
   a twisted plot
   and bad writing.
some are thick heavy tomes that
take forever to get through
    others are dainty little booklets
    with gentle words and a
    breezy style.
some are as repellent as a nasty bug spray;
you read two or three pages
and discard them quickly,
searching for a
nice
safe daily to occupy your time.
some contain profanity
others poetry.
you'll see one with a strong dependable binding,
another will fall apart at the slightest
 touch.
one might be obscure and

   impossible to understand;
another is clear as crystal, but with no
   surprises at all.
if you're lucky you find one that draws you in so
   completely
that you place it on your nightstand and keep it for
the rest of your life.
   you curl up and read it over and over again
   discovering new treasures
   each time
   around.
then you simply let your library card expire
     and thank
  God
  for
  it.

Nature's Tantrum
by Jeffrey A. Angus

The storm and its wind stumbled into the town with the attitude of a toddler who was angry.
Tossing trees, wind screaming, and the land soaked from its frustrated tears.
In its wake it left a mud puddle, debris laden landscape, much like toys spread about from a tantrum.
Days have passed and the occupants of the small coastal town emerge into the light.
The sun trying to assist the residence with the cleanup and enlighten the mood.
Stress filled days follow as the people try to restore the towns many wounds.

I walk this path I have walked before, trying to get to a place that I frequent to relax and unwind.
A light breeze blows, the tall grass waves to me like an old friend.
The leaves on the trees a symphony of sorts, the dancing breeze the conductor.
Small birds and butterflies flit through the air, hiding and moving as I pass their resting spots.
I head into the woods, the dripping water slides off the leaves disturbing nature's wildlife songs.
The Oaks weep, their territory hit harder than

others, the scars evident, strewn along the forest floor.
The storm fury evident with branches and trees laying skeletal on the damp moss covered earth.

The rocks no worse for wear, I can see my resting spot still exists.
I clean up the branches and debris, and pile them as the Vikings used to make the funeral pyre.
The forest moans, a dirge for the fallen, a sigh of thanks to its human visitor.
I read poems out loud to the forest animals, sharing some caring for the pain the storm has inflicted.
The sunshine penetrates the gloom, I walk away, back to town silently, making my way past the trees.
The forest smiles in thanks, the birds singing to pass on the message.

Seek
by Rick Ducayne

Immersed, drawn then languished,
Peopled march of woe,
Mindless, murky, worldly sea
of clashed encountered foe.

Ponderous, treasure laden chest,
Drench to plummet in,
Well meant squealing bodies,
Grieving dowsed in sin.

Beguiled as though surrounded,
Unseemly turns befell,
As craving chicks the mother hen,
The vanquished seek to dwell.

Adjoining rock- Masada,
From siege impregnable;
Crevice trimmed recessed the wall,
Their soul a citadel.

Where's the table turning?
Gallow mate's reprieve,
Lap solitary drop of hope,
All tongues would glad break free.

From it's sanctum utterance
that fallow, empty lie,
We sow the seed and sooner bleed
'fore contemplating why.

Queries swell their filling
to science also life;
True inquisitors don't sleep,
But prowl infernal night.

Is it time?
by Jeffrey A. Angus

A time to remember, my memory remains.
I feel no more pain, the medication is to blame.
A time to reflect, events from the past.
Head hung in shame, an inaudible gasp.

Is this the end? Is it over for me?
Is this just the beginning? A chance to be free?
I am a mortal man, I hate to admit.
Time may just be winning, climb into the pit.

I cry like a baby, slapped on the rump.
I laugh like a child, ticklish and plump.
I swoon like a teenager, madly in love.
I frown like an adult, society bums.

Time is winning, the bell tolls.
I am starting to get old, the story so bold.
No longer immortal, that's not the plan.
My bones ache tenfold, a regular man.

My birthday party, when I turned seven.
A big rubber ball, I kick it to heaven.
A kiss under the bleachers, her wonderful green eyes.
Hip broken in a fall, ice in disguise.

Is it my given time? Is it almost done?
Will I carry on? All out of fun?
I will pray every day, do they land on deaf ears.
Tell me I'm wrong, a vision appears.

The lights flash around me, nothing with sound.
The world is a blur, colors flash all around.
They ask me if I'm still with them. Someone starts to cry.
It is my turn, I see a deep blue sky.

I lie in the bed, nothing my own.
The radio blares on, the singer monotone.
I reflect on my life, look from above.
I hear a whisper, it's time to go, and I'm off.

Don't cry for me, I have moved on.
I am with loved ones. Who had already gone.
Keep me in your heart, a story to tell.
I will be with you, until you are called as well.

No one makes the trip to visit anymore
A waste of time, they consider me gone.
I reside here alone, only flesh and bone.
Abandoned below ground, covered in earth and stone.

Remembering When

Close Shave
(Inspired by Psalm 93)
by Rick Ducayne

w.b. yeats
delving into the dark side
of reality
deeply sinking into
occultic practices
spent years in the black arts
sorcery
sinful ritual
satanic religions
writing snake pit poetry
then by the mercy
and grace of
God
he was struck by the terror
of losing his immortal
soul
tentacles of
evil
clutching
grabbing at him

desperation erupting his
spirit
kicking out his flailing
screams of escape

NorGus Press

fleeing the fire of his demise
rescued safely in
the mass
in the church
where he stayed until
his death
another poet in heaven
by a

whisker

Remembering When

I break for sunshine
by Jeffrey A. Angus

Eyes wide open, not to be shut, a glow appears
The sunlight flows through the shades and wakes
 me from a deep sleep
I turn over trying to sink into my cave of blankets,
 my mind still in a fog
Curl into the fetal position, just a few more minutes

Welcome sunshine my old friend, thank you for
 showing up again
It may be early in the day, I may swear a bit as you
 play
The time was perfect as I forgot to set the alarm
I need to get the rest of me up and around

Every day you greet me with a smile is a good day
 for all
Bring life back to the world and shine down on us
 all
A deep breath as I step out the door
The air warm with your kiss

Morning Altar
by Rick Ducayne

he shaved with aristocratic
precision
as was his custom
short slow strokes that told of
encounters
to come that day
ritual it was
dignified moments strung together as
pearls
on the slender neck of a delicate
woman
i would gaze upward from my lowly perch
sensing the flow of
generations
in movements there
knowledge sprung from a subterranean
plane beyond conscious awareness
and a rightness
which gave birth to my first certainty
this was the initial burgeoning
right man/right place/right time
insight
which destroyed the dimly curtained
past while giving halt to musings of
the morrow
time ceased at this

Remembering When

altar
of the moment
meditating we were as deeds undertaken
and gone and those yet to
evolve
gave way with reverence
to the supreme importance of doing
this one thing right
dispassionate
errorless as the executioner pulling the
velvet cord spelling adieu
it would always be my definitive description
of peace
how far backward did it recede and then
ahead how far when the first implement struck
the first grisled cheek
while the next torch bearer
peeped and glared with workless
assent
my time was not yet
but it hovered at the doorstep outside
touching
the frayed outer edges of the welcome mat
awaiting entry
another ten minutes would
launch me
to yankees, pen knives, chain guards
and carving initials
but my days

were numbered
there was no grief in this
or joy
or apprehension
it simply stood with soldier straight back
and was satisfied with its own
inevitableness
so was i
he would glance down at unspecified intervals
and we would talk of hidden
veiled mysteries as only we two could
comprehend
the talk of men as only men can understand
those hidden treasures of the male
soul
reveling in the blatant fact of
masculinity
and then it was over
we would part till the cock crowed next
and again we'd enjoin to
the morning task
to do only this one thing
only here
only now
and to do it

right

Remembering When

The day is long but our time is short
by Jeffrey A. Angus

It's been so long, since you had gone, and it's hard to come up with what to say.
Now my time is short, and I just need support for the last few lonely days.
I sit here alone, no one to call on the phone, I take all the blame.
They don't teach you such things, and it brings life to this point today.

They didn't tell me, it would end this way, I look around and I hear no sound,
You have been gone, not very long, the hands on the clock just mock me.
As the time ridicules me as it ticks away, I wish I had more to say.
Since you've been gone, nothing is the same.

Sorry for the mess I made, Sorry for the tone I used
Sorry for the attitude and the crude way I spoke to you
It was not my intention at all, to have this happen and so
This letter is intended for you as an apology.

I look at the sky, and wonder why, I had done this once again
Everything happens for a reason they say, it's not my way
It took me a very long time, to see through blinded eyes
The things I did have not been ok.

Sorry for the mess I had made, Sorry for the tone I used
Sorry for the attitude and the crude way I spoke to you
It was not my intention at all, to have this happen and so
I leave this letter for you before I go away.

The time has come to leave this here.

Sweeper
by Rick Ducayne

In his stall he stands there tall
awaiting task and orders,
Swishing sweeping 'cross the floor
both middle space and borders.

Always faithful ever saint
his purpose keen and ready,
Smooth the handle, light to hold
with bristles strong and steady.

Think of all the countless times
you've reached for his endurance,
Rubbish strewn about the floor
he'd march with calm assurance.

As he danced through dusty webs
adrift in meditation,
We cloud our minds with sweeter times
a thankful dispensation.

Cross the line, embrace the time
when life was rife with glory,
When every day was here to stay
and told an endless story.

Through summer heat and winter's chill
his backbone stiffened for each day,
In beaming sun and darkened night
he'd make the toil just seem like play.

It's true sometimes I'd sweep some toes
and watch them running off too soon,
But blame me for it all I say
don't ever blame my blameless broom.

Ode to the phone
by Jeffrey A. Angus

That is my name, yes I know, I called you for assistance
Who are you to ask? Please identify myself? You are highly persistent.
On the other end, a cold, unfriendly voice, obviously computer generated.
No human talking to me, to them my name is not Smith, Jones, Brown, or White

Press 0, press 1, and press 2-8, I missed the prompt, I am too late.
The poor phone flies across the room in haste.
Ouch, I spent hard earned money on that thing.
Stress over a call I made, I hate the computer age.

Pick up the spare, hang my head as I hear,
Please press 1 to start over or hang up, really?
Press the button 100 times, it does not falter, I'm not surprised.
This call I made is going to give me an ulcer.

I sigh, real loud and take a deep breath, view the clouds out the window.
Or are they in my head, a storm brewing again, my phone shivers from the thought.

I start to sing the hold music between the prompt as it tells me customers are crucial to them.
I laugh and tell the automated voice what I think about it.

I have had enough, this is painful, and I have been on this call way too long.
I tap my foot, I kneed my shirt, my hair now a mess.
I look at my poor broken phone, a martyr to my rage from this call
This is Bill, how can I help you? My hand slips and I hang up.

I give up.

Slammer
(Inspired by Psalm 112)
by Rick Ducayne

"Will you be working late?" she asks.
"Depends. I don't know," he says.
Newspapers crackle.
   The room screaming with silence.
"I've decided to visit my sister for a few weeks,"
   she says.
"Seattle is just up the coast, after all."

"Sure. I mean, that's a good thing," he says.
   "Family is important."

"I'll visit her then. Guess I'll leave tomorrow
   morning," she says.

Heads are down.
Locked.

There's movement now.
He's gathering himself.
His things.
His keys.
She breaks out a list of things to pack.

He slowly makes for the door.
There's much of the room between them now.

"We could've had children," she says.
"Before I had it done to me, I mean.
We could've had a family of our own.

I'd be a grandmother by now," she says

to the
slamming

door.

Feeling the Story
by Gabrielle R. West

Can a sharp mind form meaningful words?

Can the meaningful words turn into a simple paragraph?

Can a simple paragraph turn into a heart-warming story?

Can a heart-warming story be published into the large world?

Can the world be as what we think it is?

The world has many emotions stated in its core.

Hate, Anger, Happiness, Joy and Love.

These emotions within the world is what can make a story

A story of how we feel

Life's Blacksmith
by Jeffrey A. Angus

The hammer hits the anvil with an ear piercing clang.
Over and over the hammer strikes the glowing metal.
Sparks flying as the heated metal resists the blacksmith's might.
The metal heats and finally bends to his will.

Rings made of steel, not soft gold, like others.
Our love much like the rings, the world our blacksmith.
Trials and tribulations, to strengthen our resolve.
Together we are as strong as the steel.

Our hearts beat as one as we look deep into each other's eyes.
Today love, live, eternal bonds.
We are just a cog in the wheel of life.
We will make our little piece run smooth.

Remembering When

You Devil
by Rick Ducayne

You think you see clearly.
The bricks are still in order;
still red.
Windows are boarded up as always
with filthy sooted glaze.

Then, as you scan it,
you see about half way up the block
a clump of trees protruding into space: yearning for
   the sky.
Enveloping Maples
with leafy boughs that shadow the
dirty gray streets, and a yellow
running rail up the right side.

Ugly rows of houses paint the horizon,
and beyond that, a sloping hill.

You looked on a day you believed
to be properly on the calendar.

You had no idea about timeless, tireless inversions
emerging through the cracks of asphalt lanes.

Then a lone figure moves
     across the barren street;
     deranged, defiant, dauntless.

It moves without angles:
  neither horizontal, nor vertical, nor diametrically.
It's superimposed upon the picture.
It floats closer with menace.
 The face is gaunt, frightening.
You brace yourself in terror as it floats
   into range.
It's coming to destroy you on this city street.
The features are almost recognizable now.
It picks up horrific speed and you finally see
who it is.
But it's too late.
It's the end of you.
It's you.

Remembering When

Fresh Air
by Jeffrey A. Angus

Take a breath, the air is safe.
Breath deep, fill your lungs' empty space.
Springtime fresh, fills the air.
The winter is running away in fear.
Come to the hill, sit by my side.
Watch the birds, as they fly.
The grass starting to change from brown to green
This is the first time in months it has been seen
The air still cool, when the sun goes down
Another day slips away, on this little hill we found

The veil
by Rick Ducayne

Through forests glimmered shining hue,
I walked and crunched the twiggy floor.
Enchantment swirled around my head,
And left me begging out for more.
My beast became a sweeter soul,
My howling wolf was smiling bright.
My heart was feeling like a child,
A darkened soul drawn to the light.

A siren's song was in my head,
And so I loved the elfen throng.
And swayed the leafy balmy air,
But felt that something still was wrong.
Tis then they came before my eyes,
The angels knew me by my name.
They told me secrets that they knew,
And put the devils all to shame.

The world they said beyond the veil,
Was not my plum to pluck and eat.
Just see that goodness should prevail,
And make the demons sound retreat.
Their brightness dimmed and shadows turned,
They disappeared in murky air.
So wonder not nor be alarmed,
If sometimes I should stop and stare.

Life Poem
by Jeffrey A. Angus

A life lived, not in vain
A life lived, not the same
As you or him, or she or he
A life lived, I still have much to give

A place I share, my feelings
A place I share, my knowledge
Not guarded, hidden or absurd
A place I share, in common

I am strong for your blessing
I am strong for your love
Unconditional, unrelenting, explained from above
I am strong with your guidance and your sacrifice

Who is a man, without a purpose?
Who is a man, without given strength?
Time and effort and belief in your presence
Who is a man, who is not afraid to take?

Prayer for all who share your word
Prayer for all who share your love
We give our strength to your cause
Prayer for all who share this bond

The strength of prayer, fills us all
The strength of prayer, within our halls
We guide the spirit and strengthen resolve
The strength of prayer, we give it our all

The story continues, far and wide
The story continues, we sing with pride
Voices raise and we look up high
The story continues, in your eyes.

Duck!
by Rick Ducayne

I tried to tell her that I just write
the stuff down.
Not seeking to display virtue or vice.
Not turning it into anything other than what it is.
Neither tawdry task nor enlightened endeavor.
"Mostly I'm just looking for words," I told her.
But she wasn't buying it.
"So, do you have a major influence -
you know, somebody you've tried to emulate?"
"Not really," I said.
Sometimes I can be slow in a conversation: patient;
deliberate in my paltry considerations.
This was the case as I painstakingly tried
to open her eyes - 'They have eyes, but they cannot
  see.'
"I'm always thinking about it," I say.
"Thinking about what, exactly."
"Well, everything; nothing. Looking for a feeling,
  an emotion,
a story - just thinking. Eventually something starts
  coming to life. Then
I write it down as quickly as I can before I lose it."
"Sometimes you lose it?" she says.
"Yes."
"Can you get it back?"
"Never. Once it's gone, it's gone."

"What does that feel like?" she says.
"It feels like you've betrayed something you can't know or explain. You feel grief."
"So this is serious business."
"Deadly."
"So getting back to my original question: who has been your biggest influence?"
"Daffy Duck," I finally told her.
"No, seriously."
"I am serious. I love Daffy."
She left quickly without saying goodbye.
And I had made espresso.

Mind's Eye
by Jeffrey A. Angus

Life is short, we are all aware.
Do not let it slip away, it's gone before you know.
Listen to the sound of the waves on the beach.
The breeze through the trees helps put you to sleep.
I hear a bird sing, the bees buzz on by.
A beautiful colored butterfly catches my eye.
As I sit here with you, I smile and sigh.
The most beautiful thing in nature sits by my side.

NorGus Press

Don't Cram
(Inspired by Psalm 124)
by Rick Ducayne

school(life)
is in
session

and there WILL BE
quizzes(trials) periodically

final dates(death/judgement) will be
unannounced and will vary from student
to student

so don't
count
on

cramming(final penitence)

Tides of Service
by Jeffrey A. Angus

The tide of emotions slow as the earth settles
Why did the storm settle on my home?
Give the gift of forever, retake your pride
How is it that I am always on the other side?
Clean the glass so I can see you
I see myself in you
Sending you on your way to a far off land
No longer can you be protected by my hand
Soldier of fortune, not my son
Love for his country, he's not the only one
Come home safe

Temperate Tempers
by Jeffrey A. Angus

The snow is still here, hanging in and trying to keep its foothold
Jack Frost and Father Winter plot to keep the lines of battle stable
The sun is pushing them back, the spring army struggling to free itself of the cold Earth
The terrain around us shows the scar of battle between the two adversaries.

The sunlight attacks the icicles, a glaring flash, like metal against metal
Water drips slow, as if the stalactite of frozen water is bleeding out slowly
The residents, plant and animal, turn their face up to soak in the welcome rays
A tease as the weather forecast calls for more snow, Jack and the Father win again.

Remembering When

It's Not Over
by Rick Ducayne

Don't count us out just yet
Governments have betrayed us
Politicians have sold us out like dime store dolls
Corporations plot to suck us dry
Actually not completely dry, after all
dead men can't consume.
Bankers buy wars and launder trillions back to
    themselves.
And we count body bags and run tributes
    on Sunday morning TV
But there's one thing they underestimate
    one thing they don't understand
    one thing they're too smug to fear
    the human spirit
We protect ourselves and stand our ground
We grow beards and sweat and stink and scratch
    ourselves
We cuss and spit and chew on cigars
    and we don't give a hoot
We fear no badge or uniform or rank
We love our wives and cherish our babies
Our land is our sanctuary
Our home is sacred ground
Our boys climb trees
Shoot deer
And wrestle in the grass

And we love it
We're human
We're alive
We're men
And we're not quite done yet

The Crucifix
(Inspired by Psalm 88)
by Rick Ducayne

she appeared much older than her age   this was the result of many years of the sickness that caught hold of her   not letting go   ever   not for a moment
   not even on the front porch when praying from that little black prayer book she loved with all the indulgences in it and her favorite grandchild a little blond boy with sad eyes who would play at her feet with his building blocks for hours on end   the prayer book was in large print   but still there was piercing strain in her eyes as she peered through a large magnifying glass   clicking off in her crisp mind the days and years deleted from the terrifying time she would have to spend in purgatory
   although the thought amused her that she would at least be a witness to all the shocked expressions on the faces of those who didn't believe in it   as the afternoon slowly drifted to its rendezvous with the mystical time between the worlds the time of the setting sun   dusk creeping through the windows of the enclosed porch   she would struggle with the abandonment of a life lived on the east side of city that gave her no notice and wouldn't care if she vanished into one of the envelopes that lined the kitchen table   money nicely tucked into each one with various destinations both here and abroad

missions   missions   missions   and much to the chagrin of her faithful husband pacing back and forth swearing in a combination of broken english and polish   taking umbrage with the lick of each stamp   but nobody really cared about it   not when it was time for the wrapping of her legs each day with stretch bandages   whose purpose it was to control the swelling to some extent at least   and it never worked very well   the worst part was watching her three hundred pound frame slowly dwindling   face becoming gaunt with the cheekbones more prominent now   then seeming to almost protrude right through the skin of her face
   but she still continued to laugh in the big voice that sent a shudder up the spine of anyone over the years who had the misfortune of crossing her family and paying the piper   towards the end she began to take on a glow of eternity that God gives to his children to light the path they must follow to Him   the quack doctor who had misdiagnosed her for years would come in to administer the useless needle   collect his fee in cash   and out the side door of the small frame house   funny thing was that they all thought the small blond boy was far too young to know what was happening   but he knew more about it than they did   the Holy Spirit was telling him everything   pleading with him understand   but instead the boy took on the sadness which he kept for the rest of his life   there was that

Remembering When

last time that they saw each other at the hospital
  the boy wasn't allowed inside but he would stand on the grass outside her window many stories up and she was helped to the windowsill despite the protests of those around her and they gazed at each other for brief moments that were eternal and they waved anyway this occurred on a sunshiny afternoon and not a cloud in the sky when they waved goodbye for the last time they gave the little blond boy the crucifix from her casket which hangs overlooking the threshold of his home to this day

Colors of Life
by Jeffrey A. Angus

Looking at the world sideways.
Can't take it head on.
Why are the colors so grey, black and brown?
Give me the strength to keep moving forward.
I need to see the colors of life.
Live for the day and the future and the promise it holds.
Everything happens for a reason, make that reason me.
I want to see the green, the vibrant blue.
Let me spread my wings, be one of you.
Acceptance for all, no stereotype.
Gather all together and live a happy life.

Remembering When

Ug-oh
by Rick Ducayne

In his advanced age he walked the streets,
watching them grow smaller, the neighborhood
smaller, also; the whole town seemed smaller
than it did in his distant youth. Once the lights
of the city would beckon him with singing
excitement, sprawling as it did amid the buzz
and organized confusion of a bee hive. Once
the skies appeared vast, spacious; teeming with
flighted friends, adorned with billows of sculptured
fluff by day and bedecked in jewelled extravagance
by night. Once the faces were too numerous to
safely count, and the farther he roamed from
the neighborhood, they grew unfamiliar, filled
with fresh glances and endless possibilities. But
the years long gone, and too quickly so, remained
in him a deflated rubber balloon; limp, listless,
useless, to be snatched up, stretched out, and
snapped back to the final thwack of death. Now
the city lights grew dim in the eyes so straining
to see them or even the nearest street sign. The
noise, mayhem and the city action were all
    annoyances
to unsettle his spirit, the skies closing in on him
like a vise. Now, the faces on the street are the
    same
he has passed for decades, nodding slight smiles.

Today, each one is a clear reflection of his
 advancing time
and immanent demise. Despite this, he warmed into
 echoes
of the soothing tones of a well loved melody with
 each
friendly tip of the hat, giving an ease to the step of
 his soul.
But there were some new faces now which gave
 him
the pain of uncertainty, the anguish of the
 unknown.
They appeared unrecognized, younger, stronger,
 and
they sent fear running through him for reasons
 which at first
were untouched by the reach of reason. But then
he came to know the source of the fear gripping his
 gait:
it was in the eyes. Unearthly, hard eyes devoid of
 feeling
or conscience. As if a curse had been cast by some
 witch's
brew, and also her ally, the vampire of spirit, and
 they had
sucked out their souls and left them as empty
 tombs.
The old man then came to a sound realization of
 exactly what

Remembering When

had happened: in a world gone mad with violent
    predators,
he had become

prey.

Welcome to the family
by Jeffrey A. Angus

Welcome to the family, we have waited for some time.
We hope we are ready for you, as it is your show.
Child of ours, we have watched you grow, internal love and effort.
Welcome to the world, we have been excited to see you.

Love is not a feeling, but a presence inside.
A wave of caring and understanding of one's essence.
The bell tolls for you and the ones that you love.
As we welcome in our child, bright as the sun.

Our family that grows, we add one more.
The world is your oyster and you the pearl.
This is a chance to make the necklace grow.
Bring the happiness, the joy, the appreciation of life.

A warm presence, Baby soft skin in our arms
You will be held and coddled, a gift from our love
We will do our best to bring you all your hopes and dreams
Thank you for being here and giving us the happiness of love

Remembering When

Who's Crazy
(Inspired by Psalm 79)
by Rick Ducayne

there is a man who searches for an escape or at
least some means of alleviating the stupid
senseless pain of his life   and not paying me any
attention   turns to his left to encounter a brick
wall   then to the right   another wall   forward
backward   same   up and down   wall and brick
wall he is boxed in while reading the daily mail
with all those terrible numbers   never liked
numbers anyway   very bad numbers indeed   they
rarely add up for you   unless you have a
good accountant he's thinking   realizing at the next
instant it's the least of his problems
considering at that moment all the loss of various
types   but mostly just loved ones now gone
simply disappearing into thin air and though always
anticipated is seldom without searing panic
followed by the numbing shock   the whole thing
unfolds to a beat   it's the beat   beat   beat
beat   I don't care for the words very much but it
has a good beat so I'll give it a 90   love/gone
love/gone   love/gone   and the beat goes on   thank
God for God   and it gets even worse
love/hate   love/hate   love/hate   thank God for
God again he's thinking while shaving around
the crags   contours and curves of a face lined with

resignation   an expression like that of a
bear trap about to spring shut   bloody   crunching
  deadly   his nicely ironed shirt is donned
with precision and upon grabbing the door handle
to leave for work he is suddenly on a gravel
road engulfed in the blinding light of Christ Who
thunders the words   why are you
persecuting Me   I didn't know it was You he says
  the entire truth of the Christ and the good
news of God's kingdom is then dawned upon his
mind in stunning revelation   like going to
confession after six weeks and the affable priest
turns his eyes to a menacing angle
lecturing him about his need for grace being a
family man and all   but grace is diving for deep
sea pearls and finding one is nirvana   hidden
  abandoned   but just out of reach are the holy
cards saved over a lifetime by the crazy old woman
who lived in a strange house in the middle of the
block with the overgrown garden condemned by
the board of health because of the cats   she prayed
the indulgences on the back of the cards every day
  so who's really crazy   vatican two produced
wonderful documents that nobody reads while she
prayed the prayers   do you see   and he did see the
truth of it as he fired up the chevy and headed into
the office wondering when they repaved the road to

damascus

I Fear I Will Never Know
by Jeffrey A. Angus

I fear I will never know
The joy of a cry
Witness the first breath
From a little one as it enters this world

I fear I will never witness
A first day at school
The first time excitement
A surprise of a broken rule

I fear I will never feel
My own child's hug
A whisper in my ear
From my little bug

I will not feel the pride and the joy
When they graduate high school
When they graduate college
When they start their new job

I will not see
I will not feel
I will just watch
I will be still

Cherish the times
The father-daughter dance
Your child's first laugh
Your child's new romance

I fear I will grow old and be left alone
I fear many things I'll never have known
If I see families today
I fear what it feels to be that way

Remembering When

He Sees Him
(Inspired by Psalm 45)
by Rick Dycayne

He raised You higher
than I'd seen,
with hands both strong and still.

His eyes were fixed
upon the host.
I knew it was Your will

that brought him there,
and me, as well,
my faith to strengthen bold;

this mystic priest,
the sacred bread,
the chalice lined with gold.

It seemed like an eternity
he held You in the air.

Unto this day,
I ponder still
what might have happened there.

Not once did I detect a blink,
each eyelid locked in place.

For he was gone,
no longer there
to take up earthly space.

His spirit soared,
he walked with Thee;
my Lord, I know it's true.

Oh, how I wish
upon my life
that I had been there, too.

He heard Your voice,
I'm sure of it.
I'm sure he saw Your face.

The light of God,
the Holy Ghost
descended on that place.

When it was time,
I walked with awe
and knelt down at his feet.

The body and the blood of Christ
had never been so sweet.

I'll never be the same again,
I'll see this story told;

Remembering When

the mystic priest,
the sacred bread,
the chalice lined with gold.

I fly through portals
by Gabrielle R. West

Has heaven abandoned us?
Has it left our souls to rot away in the darkness?
No, it hasn't.
Even if we don't soar through the air in hope.
Even if we don't breath in love.
Things can prevent us from being free.
Things can stop us from going down our own paths.
Things that can destroy our life.
But, that doesn't stop there, no.
It's only the beginning of our way to heaven.

Remembering When

Time is on my side?
by Jeffrey A. Angus

Time is winning
One hundred years old
My voice no longer works
The tubes grab hold

I lived a good life
Many things I recall
I have many grandchildren
I remember them all

I did see a white light
She was calling my name
The warmth replaced fear
My soul shifting from this place

I come streaming back
Light to the dark
People around me
Eyes open with a start

Let me go away
I was in a better place
I didn't feel like a fool
Let time win the race

I reunite with my love
Bathed in white light
It happened real late
A star filled night

He is gone now
Mr. Jones, Smith, or Brown
The orderly shrugs
Nobody was around

From someplace else
I watch the world continue
A smile on my face
I really will miss you

Sparky
by Rick Ducayne

"Why can't we just get along," she said.
But he was spitefully extreme in his long sneer.

"We're wasting all this time when we could be happy," she said.
But he was hateful, aroused every moment in his resentment and anger.

"Look, we could just stop right now and start loving each other."
But he was wary of it, guarded in every movement; ingenious in his disdain.

"We could skip the entire healing process and just fall in love again."
His glance reeked of sarcastic desperation. There would be no forgiving,
no pardoning, no joy.

"Can't you see we're getting older? We're going to miss our chance," she said.
His look was wearisome, yet dangerous. Like a bloodied soldier at the end of a great
battle.

"They're wrong, what they say about it. We don't need group therapy, medication or mentors.

We could just flip a switch," she said.
When he turned to her the final time, she could see
   it in his eyes.

There was a
spark.

Open Life
by Jeffrey A. Angus

A mime in life, reclusive, shyness.
Afraid to say what I feel, a shade of red.
Let it all out, send your voice into the air.
Let go, fear and trepidation.
They can read it in the tabloids.
Grow

Dusty
(Inspired by Psalm 90)
by Rick Ducayne

huddled up in
st. andrew's church was I   like
an empty chalice for the filling

semi-darkness slipped under the doors
winding around the candles

statues stately smiling
through years of pastors and nuns
and altar boys sneaking wine sips

'at the cross her station keeping'
echoed inside the silent air

the savior bled anew that evening
and faith was shed from the cross
of sacrifices unspeakable
and
thrust earthward to
torment
a sinner yet perfected
in his
craftiness and the heavenly vaults
were assailed
and
entered

Remembering When

don't tell me that I'm a good man
you who walk the streets and ride the
buses and wish me well
don't tell me about the beautiful
hands of the priest
who who knit sweaters and wrap
your legs for the pain
and die younger than necessary
don't tell me how proud you are
you who use a needle
and hug a bottle
through grimaced
and sickly smile
flesh is being ripped apart
for my sins
yet
committed
I'll revel and
stomp and howl like a wolf
gone mad
with evil starvation

can't we meet again at regular intervals
you and I
and keep the demons in suspense
while we work it all
out on paper
right there in black and white

we'll rest our case
amid the slackers and the hackers
the sailors who
slept on the couch
and the woman who tricked us without
conscience
we could indeed go on for many years in this
endeavor
like a frightened man clinging to the night's safety

and when I've sinned myself into dust
I'll return to Thee
and the love
of
st andrew's

A flash of life
by Jeffrey A. Angus

My life flashes before my eyes.
The day grows longer, but our life is short.
Can we experience everything in time?
What was the last thing I remember?
I miss the time we had spent together.
I hope you are happy and have moved along.
Had you been proud of me?

Thirsty
(Inspired by Psalm 42)
by Rick Ducayne

I thirst
and I would drink in
more of You
but
I might get filled up
overflowing
and
You would gush out of my
heart
and ears
onto the floor of the
church
and everyone will know
how much I'm crazy in love with You
and they'll think that I'm
drunk at eleven
o'clock in the
morning
not a bad idea
actually
this day could use a
little sparkle
of

You

Lunchtime
(Inspired by Psalm 114)
by Rick Ducayne

He said
come to Me and I will give you rest

is there rest in the arms of another
    only for a moment
is it right there in my portfolio
    until the dow plummets
is it found in my plans and dreams
    dashed
is it there in my memories
    only painfully
is it in my reverie
    until reality
is it in my profession
    until confession
is it hidden in nature
    better bring a lunch
how about the arts
    that's just where it starts
is it in my prayer
    you're almost there
He said
the kingdom of God is within you
a kingdom of peace
of love

NorGus Press

of justice
of grace
in the sacraments
in the

church

Donor
by Jeffrey A. Angus

Thank you for my life, I don't know what I would have done without you.
Another day to see the sun rise and hear the birds sing.
Another day to hear the kids playing outside in the sunshine.
Today is a special day; it's our joint birthday.

From tragedy comes life, life given with no regret.
I regret it had to be this way for you.
I thank you for your wish to continue on.
A part of you with me as long as I can take a breath.

A crash and boom and you had signed on the line.
Thank you and your family for taking the time.
I have the chance to live and watch my children again.
I will live, remembering you're life and your gift.

Brave
by Gabrielle R. West

I saw you standing there
Being the gentleman you are
We tried to escape this place
But she got in the way

The accident I made
You just shrugged it off like it was nothing

Until you asked me to help you
Take over this horrid place we are in
You lied

You threw me away like I was an old toy

At last, I stood in front of you brave and tall

I'll never forget the time that you

Let me go

Thinking of Melvin
by Rick Ducayne

So I'm seventeen
living in a one room flat in a flophouse
in midtown manhattan surrounded by hookers
and 'chock full o nuts' coffee shops.
I'm a copy boy at WNEW radio by night
and by day I'm feared as a cold blooded killer
by the cockroaches who also
inhabit my room.
This caused me to take long walks during the day
instead of sleeping.
One of my favorite haunts is a small
antique bookstore on 33rd street around the
corner from 7th avenue.
Instead of a sign in the window there were
giant stacks of old books.
When you walked in, the door tripped a
small tarnished silver bell which
rang out just as nice as you please.
Modest shelving peppered the walls with exotic
looking antiques that sparkled gemstone light.
There were black african warriors in full regalia, a
 large
big-nosed stone face with closed eyes
and a lion's mane.
Unusual clay pots with huge handles and obscure
 colors.

And Japanese Samurai swordsmen hand carved
out of blazing stone.
The front door was heavy glass in an iron frame.
I never saw any movement when I was looking in
   from the outside
but as soon as I entered he would quickly emerge
   from somewhere in the back.
Melvin was somewhat short with a nice build
and black hair that was slicked down with a part on
   the side.
He wore round iron rimmed glasses and a
   moustache that was high
in the middle but quickly tapered down to the
   corners of his mouth.
I never saw Melvin when he wasn't in a beautifully
   pressed suit,
creased pants, with a bright white shirt and a bow
   tie.
The only thing about Melvin that changed was the
   color of his bow tie.
Usually it was a solid muted color but sometimes
   he would
throw in a playful pattern.
Melvin would always approach me in a kind of
   walking hop step
as if he was in a hurry while always maintaining his
   dignity.
He would shake my hand and act as if the two of us
   were

Remembering When

immersed in some kind of a conspiracy. He spoke with an urgent tone
that made me feel that time was short.
"Richard," he would say,"It's so good to see you."
"You, too, Melvin," I would answer,"How have you been?"
"Oh, I've been thinking, my boy. Thinking, thinking, thinking. And I no longer
believe that the existentialists were as morbid as I previously thought."
"Maybe you're right. Maybe they were simply building a foundational paradigm
for facing life squarely."
"Good, good, you're learning. But they were still missing something, Richard."
"Okay. What?"
"Well now, that's the question, isn't it?" Let's find out together."
None of the books were on book shelves. They were all kept in neat stacks
that littered the floor, helter skelter. But all of the bindings were perfectly
lined up with not a single title upside down.
And we would wander off through the maze of book stacks.
"Here it is!" he would say. "'Existentialism: a Seminar in Reality Structures'."
The book would be half way down one of the book mountains, so we

would neatly pull it all apart, retrieve the one we wanted and then put
it all back together again. This would go on for hours: pouring over books,
journals, periodicals and magazines.
In our very first conversation he told me that I had no philosophical basis
for my thoughts. We spent the next year fixing that problem. Sometimes I'd
go in once a week, or twice a week, or three days in a row. Or I'd skip a month.
But every time I walked in we'd pick up right where we left off. From Kant and his
"Categorical Imperative" to Sartre and his blazing defence of existentialism.
From Aristotle and the roots of western thought to St.Thomas Aquinas and
his massive Summa Theologica. We delved deeply into ethics, psychology(which
Melvin believed was just this side of Voodoo), Metaphysics, Nihilism, Ontology:
Freud, Jung, Pavlov's dog, Skinner and the behavioral guys. You name it.
Then one day I was approaching the shop as I had done so many times before,
when the glass door flings open and and out bursts Melvin with a giant antique
gargoyle in his arms. He rushes past me without a word and disappeared into

Remembering When

the ocean of humanity on the noonday streets,
    never to return. I went back several times to
try to find out things but it was nothing doing. I
    never saw Melvin again.
But about once a month or so since then, I'll
    actually have a lucid thought in my head, and
now you know how it got there.

Thanks Melvin.

Tell me
by Rick Ducayne

The women want divorces
The men want whiskey
The sky wants expanses
The ground thinks it's risky
The wind wants the spirit
The soul wants the ghost
The body wants the touch
The sea wants the coast
What do you want?

Remember The Day
by Jeffrey A. Angus

I stand in the dark - silent and cool - a calm autumn day
Relaxed, listen to the rhythmic sounds of the ocean waves
A dark void unseen, but a few feet away
The Darkness laughs as the sounds carry in the wind - a bird - I hope.

On the edge of darkness, a sliver of hope
A glow, an intrusion into the darkness
It gets brighter as I watch the dark shy away
The waves rolling towards the shore.

A wind picks up, pushing away the darkness, chilling the bone
The sun now cresting the horizon, welcoming a new day
Scent of the sea, I close my eyes to a time when it was not just I here but *we*
Love life as it brings another day, wish you still stood with me.

Shoppers
by Rick Ducayne

There's no contentment we all say
in what we have; we want much more
of all there is to buy today -
we all must shop in every store.
And when we think we have enough
of happiness we get from things,
we long to get a lot more stuff
and own the emptiness it brings.

Slappy
(Inspired by Psalm 69)
by Rick Ducayne

I said the stations of the cross that day
And the anguished laundered through the ringer
Sheets of my brain mixed themselves with the passion
  of Our Lord.
Somewhere around the third fall of Christ a little old nun
(not one of these new fangled deals in street clothes so
you can't tell them from the grocer's wife)
In a full black habit complete with wide starched expanses
bordering a weathered wise face with high beams coming
  at you directly,
Approached and told that she perceived I had a special
Devotion to the stations of the cross and that when I died
Jesus would come for me Himself.
I stammered something inane about how special I thought
I was, too, but she had already turned on her heel and was gone,
No doubt disappointed,

While I awkwardly withdrew in the knowledge that
 I hadn't
Yet lost my touch for seizing an otherwise sacred
 moment
And slapping it silly.

Remembering When

Normal Life Alone
by Jeffrey A. Angus

A normal man he lives alone
A world he wished he had never known
The times are changing, why has he not?
Most of his friends are in prison or have been shot.

A normal man still lives alone
He watches the world drift past his home
It moves at a pace he can't understand
Most days he feels he's in another land.

A normal man still lives alone
The world around him, he looks and moans
Why is society twisting its hand?
What does it mean to be a man?

What is normal anymore?
Alone, but not, society invades his home
Gunshots and stabbing everywhere, hang your head in despair
Society is in chaos, it's not clear, why it's happening, it's not fair

Normal living, I am alone
I don't understand the assault on our own
Time bombs ticking, what to do?
The next victim could be me or you.

Survived a war many forgot
I live next to a dealer, a drug hotspot
I try to make my business my own
The violence encroaches on my safe place, my
    home

A normal man he lives alone
A world he wished he had never known
The times are changing, why is he not?
Most of his friends are in prison or have been shot.

Remembering When

Buckle up
(Inspired by Psalm 39)
by Rick Ducayne

Fasten your seat belts,
The ride isn't long;
You think it's forever,
You blink and it's gone.

You wake in the morning,
It's your fist day of school;
A couple weeks later
You're a crinkled old fool.

It's often perplexing,
The whole thing sped by;
The dreams of a lifetime
Reduced to a sigh.

We search for some meaning
To make it worthwhile;
Some faint consolation
Before the last mile.

But life has one object,
Just one to achieve;
The will of the Father,
Then it's time to leave.

NorGus Press

To be there with Jesus
In heavenly spheres;
Goodbye to all heartaches,
Goodbye to all fears.

Remembering When

My Own Score Keeper
by Jeffrey A. Angus

Don't give up, work hard to make things happen.
If we only look into ourselves, we can gather the strength we need to succeed.
A place of comfort, joy and happiness can be found.
We have it within ourselves to make it back to that place.
A space we build to put our trophies, life and accomplishments we gather.

Society can push you back, keep you down, not everyone is the same.
You are who you are for a reason, no-one but you can judge.
Be real and honest to yourself and accomplish the goals you set.
You have the only score card, keep your scores for your life your own.
You have made it this far, you are ahead in every category.

Find time to be you, express your feelings, and ignite your passions.
Bring to the table your best, show your style and swagger outward.
Life it is a complex equation, do the math, it will

add up to success
As long as you are ok with you, then nothing else matters

Not a Word
(Inspired by Psalm 105)
by Rick Ducayne

it's like when Abraham
took Isaac
to the
mountain of sacrifice
and once
there
tied the boy
placing him on the altar
and raised his
dagger
to plunge it into
the heart
of his
son
in obedience to the
will of God

but God stopped Abraham
from killing
Isaac
and provided
a sacrificial substitute
instead

well
the bible doesn't record
a single word spoken
between Abraham
and Isaac after
this ordeal

not one more
word
between father and
son

sometimes
we can survive
something
but it
doesn't mean things
go back to the
way they

were

We Aquarius
by Gabriel West

We, Aquarius, are unnoticeable
But, we try to have a voice

We, Aquarius, have no emotions to show
Only, if we are not alone

We, Aquarius, can make things happen
only if we are here to help other zodiac's

We, Aquarius, can change everything
And everyday

Poet's View
by Jeffrey A. Angus

"To be a poet is a condition, not a profession."
            ~ Robert Frost

I have been labeled, by more than one being.
I have been noticed for things I have seen.
The way the words flow from my mind is unique.
I look around and see so many people looking at
    me.

A window into the soul, the words just tend to
    flow.
I see the same thing different each time I go.
Time is of the essence, time is on my side.
Express what you feel, your soul tells no lies.

I will not be given insurance, a raise or steady pay.
My parents scowl and glare and shake heads.
This is not a profession in this day and age.
That prose and the art has to be dead.

I beg to differ, as I have so much to show.
Love, life, experience and the places I go.
Look on the page, read and hear the words.
In my life it is still vital to give back to people on
    earth.

Quiet Love
A Short Story by Rick Ducayne

It was always said of John and Nancy Woodman that they were a handsome couple. And it was still true after fifty-two years of a mostly happy marriage. Anyway, they had fared better than most of the couples they had known over the years. The Dutch Colonial house, their dwelling for thirty-plus years, still stood the test of time; its stone walls a fortress, its steep roof a beacon in the staunch, middle class neighborhood in which they had raised their family of seven children. There would have been more, but Nancy's body began to break down after losing the last two shortly after childbirth. So seven it was, four girls and three boys, and it was plenty they had concluded, back in the day when the kids were all home. The diapers, the doctors, the prescriptions, glasses, dentists, report cards, teacher's conferences, softball, little league, soccer, basketball, cheerleading, Ukrainian Dance, altar servers, plays, musicals, dances, proms, swimming, fishing, sibling rivalries, boxing; and that was just for the first three kids. Life was full, rich with meaning and purpose. They never had to search for themselves or wonder what to do with their time. But the wheel had turned, and their current situation was decidedly different. Everyone was long since out of the house; scattered throughout the entire American landscape. From California to Alabama, up into the breadbasket, then over to New England. Their children, now grown into their own families, seemingly everywhere but home. Even the second youngest, with her husband and family of five children who lived only 45 miles east along the New York State Thruway, seemed light years away. Sure there were many letters, numerous long-distance phone calls, a torrent of emails, visits and family get-togethers. They had warm loving relationships with all their grandchildren, having every reason to settle into a cozy and satisfied final stage of their lives. This, however, was not the case. John was never much of a television viewer and had grown bored with golf, poker and woodworking. He was now ill content with his favorite pastime of sitting on the front porch watching the world go by. Nancy wasn't doing much better. The sewing machine in the far corner of the back enclosed porch showed some cobwebs on the spindle. Her embroidery supplies lay scattered on a wonderful Victorian mahogany dresser nearby. Thus, she had taken to wandering about the house in a more or less aimless search for something worthwhile to do.

And so it had come to this on a somewhat overcast Sunday morning with faint hints of muffled sunlight trying desperately to give comfort to those in need, but unsuccessful. The diffused light cast a spell in the house that was contagious. John was seated in an armchair dressed in a dark gray cardigan sweater, the last two buttons undone with a pouch of pipe tobacco in the side pocket. This covered a crisp white dress shirt, finished off with pleated dress slacks and polished black shoes.

"It's so quiet," she said.

"Yes," he said. "I hate it."

He couldn't help but notice that his wife had maintained a slim figure and erect stature as she walked across the room. She was attractively attired in a bright printed dress and not quite sensible shoes with a bit of a heel. Stopping at a small end table, she picked up a small lamp.

"This is real porcelain. Got it as a wedding gift.

Remember, Darling?"

"I can't remember what I had for breakfast."

"I was always so afraid they would knock this over someday, but I refused to put it away. I wanted to leave something beautiful out in the open where I could see and enjoy it. You know what I mean? I was always hollering at them to get away from that table, don't play near the lamp. They never did break it. Then when they didn't know I was within earshot I could hear them mimicking me. 'Get away from that lamp...Get away from that lamp.' Then they would all laugh and I'd be around the corner laughing, too. It all seems so silly now. You never took their side though. You always backed me up on everything."

"Well, like you always said - it was them against us," he said noticing the soft tears welling up in his wife's eyes. Then John Woodman rose from his chair, walked the length of the room, and putting his arm softly around her shoulders, did his best to quell the storm of loss that he knew they were both feeling. They were standing adjacent to a long table on which sat a wonderful collection of photographs in various shapes and sizes; some of them beautifully framed in ornate workmanship, others held by simple straight wooden frames.

"Look," he said. "Jack's First Holy Communion. He did such a wonderful job. We were so proud of him. Handsome boy."

"Of course, he's handsome. They're all beautiful. Here's Sarah and Brian receiving their confirmations together. So many people were against it because of the difference in their ages," she said with a chuckle. "But Father Eli would have none of it. He said they both knew their faith and were more than ready. But then he always went his own way."

"He always went the way of the church."

"Yes, you're right."

Nancy picked up another picture, gazing at it through misty eyes.

"Here they are in the pool. Remember how endless the summers were back then. Time seems short now. I feel like I'm on fast forward."

"Do they still have a fast forward?" he said.

"Who knows anymore. I do know that you're the only one I can think of who still plays tapes."

"Never mind about that. The VCR still works fine and besides that I like those movies."

It seemed that many of their conversations were now riddled with bitterness, a vague emptiness that clouded their minds and darkened their days. But, to be sure, there was no falsehood or deceit between them. Honesty had been the bedrock of their marriage. This they continued to foster even in their pain; especially in their pain. It was only a week ago when he had awakened to find her sitting on the side of the bed sobbing into an endless supply of tissues now scattered across the floor. It was then that they commenced sharing those thoughts and feelings which, although not completely understood, created in them a certain resolve and sense of togetherness. Why they hadn't begun this cleansing process earlier they did not know, but now was now and the loss of their children's childhood became clarified, if not hopeless. It occurred to both of them that what was a burdensome life to so many other couples had been sheer joy for them. Nancy felt a chill run up her spine as they talked and decided to go upstairs to their bedroom to fetch her robe. John drifted off to the back porch, and after making some pale efforts to tidy up, decided it was hopeless and best left for another day.

Remembering When

Seating himself on a long glider, he could hear keenly the laughter and voices of each of his children as they all sat right there in his arms looking out into the backyard. Life, he decided, was filled with an endless series of natural circumstances which were out of his control. There was life, death, and all the rest in between. Suddenly he saw in his mind's eye his daughter Patricia with her beautiful hazel eyes: enchanting, innocent. He noticed the gold wristwatch he was wearing; a birthday present from three or four of them, he couldn't remember which ones. They had worked odd jobs over summer vacation, pooling their funds. Shortly thereafter, his wife Nancy joined him on the glider, and they sat together rocking gently, back and forth, reminiscing over a life they had chosen, now slipping away by the hour, by the minute, by the second. There was no amount of conversation which they could undertake to remove the silence which screamed at them constantly. Nancy watched as the countenance of her husband, once so kindly, so self-assured, was transforming into the face of a stranger. This struck her with no small amount of fear. She told her husband they were sorely in need of a cup of tea and rose to make some, pronto. He followed her into a tidy kitchen with freshly painted walls, clean floors and a lovely kitchen table she had gotten from her mother. It had been in the family for generations.

"Hey, wait a minute," he said. "Are you telling me that everything was always perfect around here?"

"No... no... I'm just saying that it seems like it now, looking back."

"Well, there must have been plenty of imperfections that our memories are discarding."

"I'm sure you're right. I just can't think of any right now."

The doorbell was singing out before she finished the sentence. They swiftly marched the length of the house to the front door to see about this most unusual disturbance. They opened the door to a woman of medium height, but right stout as can be. Her face was making every effort to be cordial while maintaining a bright reddish glow. She held by the hand a small boy, maybe seven years old, wearing a striped turtleneck shirt and shorts that came halfway up muscled little legs of steel. Every inch of his face seemed covered in freckles, his neon red hair tousled over his ears and forehead.

"Hi folks!" the lady said. "I'm Sadie Haverson from two doors down. Remember we moved in three months ago? You brought over a fresh baked apple pie, Mrs. Woodman. Well, anyway, here I am in a terrible fix having to run off to Towerton to help my brother Vernon move out of a second-story apartment which, would you believe, I plum forgot all about. And then Vern just got so upset with me on the phone 'cause others aren't showin' up neither. So like I said, here I am and there's no way a responsible parent like myself could inflict that ride both ways upon a small child. What's he gonna do while I'm haulin' furniture all day, I ask myself. We already know all about you folks from the others hereabouts: how you raised all them kids of yours, and how kind and understanding you always are with folks in a fix, such as myself at the moment. And it would just be for some hours from now till I help Vernon get himself moved. He's a good boy mostly. Needs some watchin' sometimes, but I can't imagine you'll have much trouble with all your experience and such. So here he is then and don't worry about the food and like that. We'll get all squared up when I get back."

With that, Sadie Haverson handed her son to the Woodmans, who had been standing there dumbfounded by her speech and manner.

"What's his name?" Nancy called out to her neighbor who was quickly climbing back into a black SUV.

"Woody," she shouted through the sound of peeling tires. "We call him Woody."

Just at that moment, the boy broke away from John's grip and raced to the rock garden in front of the house, grabbed up a good one, and chucked it at the bird house perched atop a pole in the middle of the front lawn. It was a direct hit, would you know, and ripped off a large piece of the overhanging roof.

"It looks like our babysitting fee has just gone up considerably," John said.

"Now, now, he's just a boy," Nancy said. "He may need a little direction, but this is our chance to do something nice for someone." As she talked, Nancy was running as best she could around the birdhouse and through much of the front lawn, till she finally caught the little speedster as he was doing laps around and in front of her. She gasped for breath, heaving as she struggled to hold him.

"You know something young man," John said. "That birdhouse has been up on that pole for thirty years. And in the whole time I've never had to repair it. You ought to be ashamed of yourself, Woody."

"Don't call me Woody! My name is Rambo. I must fire my grenade launcher whenever I see enemy planes. All us soldiers do it."

"What do you know about Rambo or grenade launchers?"

"I know plenty. My dad plays the Rambo movies all the time. He lets me watch most of them, but sometimes he makes me close my eyes until he gives me the okay."

"Sounds like you've got a pretty smart dad, Rambo."

"Sure do," Woody said, tracking huge globs of wet mud across the living room carpet on his way to the kitchen. If John hadn't known better, he would swear he could see the little leprechaun mushing down the mud a little extra. But he dismissed it as his imagination.

They talked more about Rambo-type things, including missing POWs in Vietnam and also in other parts of the world. The boy said he was hungry in a tone that suggested that he hadn't eaten in a week, but the Woodmans sensed that it was rather his perpetual state. Because it was always good policy to keep children well fed and also to keep him quiet, Nancy rolled out a lunch fit for a four-star general. There was fried spam and toast, crisp bacon, butter fried potatoes and freshly baked cherry pie. They watched in awe as the youngster polished off every morsel, washing it down with two big glasses of milk. The only bad part was one broken plate and a broken glass that went down when he was scanning the kitchen for viet cong.

As they took turns vacuuming and sweeping up the broken glass scattered everywhere you looked, the doorbell rang once again. It was their daughter Denise who lived up the Thruway.

"Look, I know I should've called first, but I just had to get things rolling out of the house, and then once we were on the road I couldn't use the phone, and I didn't want to pull over and lose time."

"You want us to watch some kids," John said with

Remembering When

resignation.

"It's Jim's kidney stones. They're back with a vengeance. I've already got him admitted back home, but I had nowhere else to turn for the kids."

"So you came all the way out here?" Nancy said.

"What else could I do?"

"Okay. How many do you want us to watch?" John said.

"All five."

Denise waved her arms toward the station wagon parked at the far end of the driveway, signaling her children who came flying out of more doors than anyone knew a station wagon had.

They descended upon grandma and grandpa en masse practically bowling them over with love, affection, and now that mom was back in the station wagon and leaving town, FREEDOM!

Woody and the kids hooked up right quickly and were now six strong. John pointed out to his wife that it was now six against two. He didn't like the odds. Well, before you could say 'Mob Rule', they scattered themselves throughout the house like rats. Little Stevie shouted out at the top of his lungs, "The Indians are comin' round the corner, boys. Let's get ourselves upstairs in the bedrooms where we can put up a good fight!" A bunch of them, you couldn't tell just how many, pounded up the stairs whooping and hollering Indian war calls. A few minutes later, they came galloping down the stairs like stampeding horses, then back up again and so on. Nancy Woodman felt sure her house would cave in at any moment. The five grandchildren were three boys and two girls. Neither of the girls had begun to grow into their femininity and to say they were tomboys would be a gross understatement. Anyway, the older of the two had gathered all the pillows and cushions she could find in the downstairs and had taken to flinging them at anyone within range. She was a good shot and two of her missiles had knocked people off their feet. She would then quickly gather up her ammo and begin another barrage, which she decided was great fun. There was some collateral damage, however; one vase, half the framed pictures, not to mention the front drapes.

The younger of the girls, Janie, stood in the middle of the melee, observing, gathering her thoughts. At last, she struck upon that thing which gave her so much delight at home: playing with food. And so she tapped into a burst of energy and sprinted into the kitchen. Unfortunately, before she got there one of her brothers sped around the corner and they collided. Janie inflicted the worst damage as she inadvertently head-butted her brother in the nose. He countered by bleeding profusely all over the new beige carpeting.

Now, you may wonder, where were our heroes whilst all these joyful events were transpiring.

Make no mistake of it they were extremely active, covering much ground, vocalizing as they went; barking out orders, giving stern reprimands and otherwise ruling the roost: all to no avail. At the moment, Nancy Woodman was stuffing tissues up the bleeder's nose, while trying to recall how much blood one can lose before losing consciousness. John Goodman was attempting to separate the cowboys from the Indians, but had gotten sidetracked by the youngest grandson, Mark, who had wet his pants along with the entire back porch, and was now screaming out for aid. In the meantime, Janie -- you remember Janie -- she watched her brother bleed for awhile in fascination before proceeding into the kitchen. It took several minutes of rummaging around but she finally located a tub of chocolate frosting in the refrigerator, proceeded to pop it open thinking it was a swell idea to finger paint her ABCs all over the freshly painted walls.

It was then that the doorbell rang again. It was a reluctant Nancy Woodman who slowly opened the door. There stood in her doorway a pleasant man of great stature with, would you believe it, a child by the hand.

"Hello," said the man, smiling broadly. "I'm Mel Haverson from up the street. You know, with the pie, and all that. You've got my kid and don't we appreciate all you're doin' to get us through this day. Quite a little shaver ain't he. Well, anyway, there I am and helpin' out the brother-in-law with movin. Man, does he have some stuff for one guy, and heavy as heck, too.

"But anyway, there I am movin' dressers down two flights and up on the truck, and I get the call from the other sitter, you know, we broke up the two boys so as not to place too heavy a burden on any one person, and she gets a headache or something and can we pick him up, so I leave the crew to gather him and where else can I go being new in town and all, and it would only be a couple more hours, your having Woody already. So here you go and thanks." Mel Haverson places his boy's hand into the numbing hand of Nancy Woodman and leaves in a flash. 'Seven', she thought. 'Seven against two....again.' She led the boy into the house, caught sight of her husband out of the corner of her eye. He was pulling apart two cowboys who had gotten into it over the last cookie out of the cookie jar. The cookie jar was nowhere to be seen and John had just given up on it. His attention was drawn to the new youngster Nancy was hauling in.

"Another one?" he said. "What's his name?"

"Who knows?"

John's head throbbed like a budding explosion. The noise in the house had reached decibels that only dogs should be able to hear. He glanced at his wristwatch. WOW! Hours had gone by. These kids haven't eaten anything.

Suddenly, there was a blood curdling scream to his right. Quickly he turned, ready to pounce. It was Nancy who was sprawled out on the rug, her arms out stretched, holding the porcelain lamp, still intact.

Standing nearby was Woody. "What? I didn't mean it," he said.

John took the beloved lamp away from her and replaced it on the table. Helping Nancy up, he ushered her over to an armchair; her eyes blank, her spirit broken.

"Okay, everybody, it's time to eat! C'mon now, time to eat! That's right; that's right! Here we go!" he screamed. They came from everywhere: from under the beds upstairs, the bathrooms, broom closets, under tables, and behind drapes. After corralling them all into the kitchen, Mr. Woodman began a distribution of food that, though unorthodox, would be the envy of any restaurant or supermarket. He had them seated at the kitchen table, the counter, and even dragged in some chairs from other rooms. Then it began. I won't say he threw the food at them, but it was more throwing than serving. Out it came from the cupboards and pantries: cookies, doughnuts, crackers, peanut butter, milk and cereal, toast, frozen waffles, peanuts and olives. Yes, olives. Some grabbed a plate, some a napkin; others just ate on their laps. They tried some of this and then exchanged it for some of that. Potato chips, raisins, butter and hamburger rolls. They put together food combinations as yet unknown to man. That was Round One.

"Hey, you got any ice cream?" blasted out one of the girls, over the clattering uproar.

That marked the beginning of Round Two. John found two five-quart tubs: one in the freezer upstairs, one downstairs. There were plenty of syrups left over from New Year's Eve: chocolate, strawberry, pineapple, and caramel. Even whip cream and crushed nuts. It was a free for all. As the second container of ice cream neared the bottom, John could begin to sense a change in the room. The noise level had gone from deafening to only slightly painful. That's what made it possible for him to hear the doorbell ringing once again. Passing through the living room he saw his wife, still in the armchair, showing hints of life. That was a good sign. When he opened the door, he noticed that the day had fallen into early evening. Where had the time gone? It was their daughter, Denise.

"Sorry it took so long, Daddy. Jim is fine. They've got him on an IV and a lot of morphine. He's actually kind of cute doped up. Well, never mind. C'mon everybody, time to go."

As the five of them came out of the kitchen, piling into the station wagon, she thought they looked a little strange. Colorful around the edges: pink and blue and even green. Also one very red nose. Well, whatever. Waving goodbye, they turned off the driveway and were gone.

When John went back into the house, Nancy was up and gingerly moving around with her head in her hands. They both made their way into the kitchen where Woody and his unnamed brother were finishing off the ice cream, but moving considerably slower. The kitchen looked like the aftermath of a food fight between the Green Bay

Packers and the Chicago Bears.

You guessed it: doorbell.

Mrs. Haverson.

"Finally got back. The move went great. Mel stayed to have a couple with the men. You know how they are. Anyway, the bed is put together, dressers in place and all the hard parts are done. How were the boys? They're quite the pair, aren't they? Thank goodness you're here with all that experience with kids, and so kind and willing to help people, and all. Let's go, boys. Say thank you. Get in the truck now. Thanks again; I can't tell ya. Let's square up for the watching and the feeding and all?"

John Woodman turned back, surveying the carnage inside. Then he turned again to face Mrs. Haverson.

"It's on the house," he said.

Mumbling her appreciation as she walked away, Mrs. Haverson jumped into her SUV and started home.

John and Nancy Woodman closed the door and stood there motionless. Eventually, they began moving about the house. Nancy made tea while John cleaned up the living room. When they were seated together on the sofa, they both gave out a simultaneous sigh of relief. They sat there in the silence for a long time.

"It's so quiet," she said.

"Shhhhhhhh," he said. "I love it."

Remembering When

The Searching Self
A Short Story by Rick Ducayne

Candles flickered dimly through the darkened church as Father Zak strolled gently up the center aisle to the tall, thin figure of a woman, who stood motionless awaiting him at the doors to the vestibule. The darkness wrapped itself around him and made him seem to be moving in slow motion. As he walked, the woman's face drew into clear, sharp lines, with hazel eyes that caught sparkles from the dancing wicks of flame. Joan Walker was 27 years old, but she looked older. She'd journeyed some considerable distance on this night to reach the small Catholic Church carved deeply into the downtown asphalt of the small city. Around them, the whizzing madness of urban racket had reduced to a blanket of city silence that calmed the spirit and quickened the senses. It was the chilly spring rain that she had let in the front doors which alerted the good father that he had a late night visitor.

He reached the last pew while stretching out his right hand in a reserved gesture of goodwill. The strawberry blond-headed girl reciprocated, and as they shook hands the faint hint of a smile curved itself around Father Zak's face.

"Welcome to St. Stephen's," he said.

Father Zak had been praying the Divine Office before the Blessed Sacrament. This was his custom each night before retiring to the rectory across the walkway. He was one of the few priests probably left in the world who continued to pray the sacred prayers in Latin, which was and always had been the official language of the Catholic Church. On some nights, when so inspired, he would even sing some of the responses in Gregorian Chant. But on this night he had been interrupted from the almost mystical altered state of consciousness he achieved when praying alone before Our Lord in the tabernacle. However, he was not in the slightest bit aggravated or disappointed. Over the many years of his priesthood, he had learned that Divine Providence could, and often would, place within his path people or circumstances which could demand his immediate attention. And so it was on this night, with the young woman standing before him from whom he expected a response. A response that was not immediately forthcoming. Instead, she gazed at him with a hint of helplessness in her expression. Her body was long and taut but revealed a hint of weakness, of vulnerability. She leaned against the pew, giving out a warm sigh of deep relief, as if she were in a raging storm at sea and had just been plucked out of the deadly waters and placed safely upon a sturdy bark.

"Hello, Father Zak," she finally said.

The good father did a quick appraisal of his visitor; something he was very good at after having honed these skills over his twenty plus years as a Catholic priest. But in all his experiences he had never encountered quite the site which stood before him on this dreary, wet night. The rain pelted the stained glass windows as if outside forces propelled themselves against the small church; driving relentlessly to break through and infiltrate the serene darkness with their evil designs.

Although the girl was overly lean and unsteady on her feet, her frame showed the solid strength of an athlete who had been weakened under a gargantuan strain. He saw in her face nothing like despair, but a deep faith that had been laid to waste by... by what? This was what he must discover as soon as possible if he was to be of some use in

Remembering When

whatever the circumstances might be.

"You know my name," he said.

"Yes. St. Stephen's was listed in a brochure I happened across. You were named as the pastor of the church. It described you as a traditionalist priest."

Father Zak let out a muffled laugh. "That must've been an old brochure," he said. "Things have changed quite a bit in the church since that was printed. These days we so-called traditionalists have gone underground, so to speak."

"Underground? How is that possible?"

"For our purposes, on this night, let's just say we're somewhat out of the mainstream of things. Our funding is private and our benefactors are also generous to the diocese: so the bishop looks the other way."

Father Zak continued to consider her quietly up and down, and deep into the pools of her eyes which she had trained on him, like double barrels from a quick shotgun. 'And no less dangerous,' he thought.

"So here we are," he said.

"Yes," she said.

The girl then walked over to the side aisle, straight to one of the fourteen magnificent oversized stations of the cross hanging hulk-like over her, ready to pounce.

"Jesus is laid in the tomb," she said, turning to Father Zak in polite deference.

"Yes. The ordeal is over, the journey has reached its final destination, and in three days, the resurrection in His eternal glory. What about you?"

"What do you mean?"

"Where are you in your journey?"

The woman shot a laser glance back toward the vestibule. "I'd say somewhere down there in the middle.

Still carrying my cross; still falling."

"And still getting back up again. In the meantime, you have me at a disadvantage. You know my name but I...."

"I'm sorry, Father," she said, giggling with femininity. "My name is Joan Walker."

This set them off into a flight of conversation. There was give and take, sharing of thoughts and insights. Father Zak was an accomplished, acknowledged master at drawing out the secret caverns of a person with sleight-of-mind dexterity and the precision of a surgeon. The young woman proved up to the task, however, and with deft remarks in a vivid, artful vocabulary, she was able to tell her story respectfully, but without revealing more than necessary to justify her arrival at St. Stephen's on this bleak, stormy night. Even as she talked, Joan Walker's deeper mind noticed the thread that ran through the length and breadth of her life. It was a seeking, searching, wandering about; not aimlessly but wandering nonetheless, in search of a nameless fulfillment of that emptiness she had known most of her young life. Father Zak had provoked a surprisingly clear review of her childhood, adolescence and maturity into young womanhood.

As they talked, the two tall, thin figures began to walk up the left side aisle of the small, ornate, gothic interior of the most beautiful church she had ever seen.

"There are those people, Father, who say we shouldn't spend money on churches like this. They say it's money ill spent. They say the money could have been given to the poor instead."

Father Zak was smiling when he said, "The only reason that beauty exists is because God exists. No one has to go to a seminar to know that the setting of the sun over a

Remembering When

body of water, in all its resplendent color and majesty, is a thing of beauty. All of us know when something is truly beautiful. That's because we are made in the image and likeness of God, and God is beauty. So it's only natural that we should design and build a beautiful house for Jesus in the tabernacle. Nothing is too good for him."

Joan listened intently as they strode past a series of kneelers that lined the outer perimeter of the church. And on the wall adjacent to each kneeler hung a colorful plaster likeness of a saint with a short inscription underneath. Halfway up the aisle, they came to the place of St. Philomena. Joan abruptly stopped, frozen, as if in alarmed joy: her face bright with anticipation, as the flickering candlelight of the church showed bright her countenance.

"Who is that, Father?" she asked, her mind wondering at the correct pronunciation.

"That's St. Philomena. Fill-o-meen-a," he said. "Her story is particularly inspiring. She was horribly murdered by a Roman ruler during the earliest days of the church for refusing to relinquish her virginity to him. She was very young. The church has given her the title 'Powerful with God.' Why do you ask?"

"I feel drawn to her," Joan said, glancing from the image of the great saint back to the open expression on the face of Father Zak.

"That's a good sign, my dear. A good sign indeed," he said. He pretended not to notice that she had revealed to him at that moment the deepest yearnings of her heart. The void of emptiness which lay within her; the desperate quest upon which she had embarked.

"I'm staying in a little bed and breakfast up on the hill, going east out of town," she said.

As they reached the front of the church, Father Zak

turned and said, "What has brought you all the way from…"

"Johnson City," she said.

"Yes," said Father Zak. "Johnson City. What has brought you all the way from Johnson City to St. Stephen's, Joan?"

"Well, it's kind of odd, Father. After all the heartache, the pain, and the loss that I've been through, all the brokenness in my family, abandonment by the people I loved and trusted, brokenness in my personal relationships, and all the rest, I'm actually here because some people I know had set me up with a blind date, and I just couldn't go through with it. So, here I am."

"Do you mean to tell me that you're here because you're running away from a blind date?"

"Yes. That's exactly what I'm telling you."

"Well, you came to the right place. Morning mass is at 7:30 sharp. Can I expect you?"

"You can. Good night, Father."

He bade her good night, watching as she walked through the heavy doors of the church. He remembered the long years of seemingly endless battles he had fought to find himself in this position as pastor of St. Stephen's.

It was late when he locked the church, taking the short walk across the grounds to the brick rectory which was his residence and prayer fortress. These walls shielded him from a world gone mad in so many ways. This was where he prepared himself for battle. However tender and lofty his speech might be, Father Zak always carried with him the scars from many years of struggles during which he fought valiantly against the satanic forces of evil which sought to rip apart the very muscles and tendons of the universal church, now over 2000 years old. It had all led him to St. Stephen's; a place of truth and hope to those in despair; to those who needed help, and Joan Walker was definitely someone who needed help. And from the look of things, a lot of it. When she first appeared, he could see an air of breeding about her, a certain strut in her step, which spoke of strength and authority. But he soon noticed, as they eased into their conversation, that she was a woman who had grown up under many varying influences. This became apparent when, during their talk, she began to make a serious turn-about from an independently self-assured woman to someone who harbored secret thoughts and motives. These demanded her attention, propelling her to seek lasting, meaningful solutions to her life. He sensed that she wasn't searching for herself as much as she was searching for someone else. Who it might be he did not know, but the force of her quest was formidable, as was the strength of her resolve to answer the questions tormenting her weary heart.

    Through these two decades of his priesthood, Father Casey Zak had seen the vicissitudes and tormented turmoils which can haunt the human soul and psyche. At first he would smile smugly, even disdainfully at the trifling cares and obvious weaknesses that seem so painfully prevalent in his fellow man. In his own life, however, he himself began to feel the sting of petty contrivances, disturbing attacks of rivals and jealous contemporaries, which turned the tide of his feelings for the plight of others. As he fought valiantly against the evil forces of modernism threatening the very foundation of the church, he could feel himself being groomed for the task which became his mission in life: leading others out of whatever darkness that had descended upon them, into the light of truth, life and challenge awaiting them on the other side. This he had sworn to do in a pact with his Creator. If others could sell their souls to the devil, he would offer his soul to Almighty God. This, he realized from the beginning, was by no means an easy task. Against him came flinging in wild rage all the forces of hell, both spiritual and natural. But with him always was the sword and strength of truth. Those things which once had offended him in others, now became his springboard to a purposed life and eternal salvation. As he turned the lights off in the rectory, he thought of these things and of Joan Walker. Could he delve into her secrets deeply enough to effectually help her: and help her in what way? What was the nature of the torment so clearly written across the face of her soul? 'Tomorrow then,' he thought. 'Tomorrow.'

The next morning the skies remained overcast, sprinkling a light drizzle upon the grounds of St. Stephen's. Father Zak took the walk from the rectory to the church in quick steps, noting the vehicles lined up in the parking lot to the side and along the curb in front. The congregation of St. Stephen's, while relatively small, was devout and faithful. Masses, including early morning, were well attended. Father Zak was attended by four altar boys in the small room, or sacristy, to the left of the altar. They proceeded with a daily ritual whereby the altar boys assisted him in putting on the beautiful, ornate mass vestments over his own clothing. The boys were already dressed in traditional cassocks and surpluses, pressed and starched to perfection, undoubtedly by devoted mothers, who were proud to have their boys upon the altar, so close to the tabernacle. This might foster a special devotion to the faith and possibly result in a vocation to the priesthood. One never knows.

The boys properly held in their hands at certain

points in the procedure various vestments that Father Zak would wear when he emerged from the sacristy to the altar. These included the Amice: a white linen cloth which he wore around his neck and shoulders, to symbolize the helmet of salvation or trust in Jesus Christ; the Alb: which was a long white linen garment reaching to the feet, symbolizing purity; the Cincture: or white cord worn around the waist, which was also an emblem of purity. And so it went through various other carefully chosen and meaningful garments, until finally he was adorned with the Chasuble, the outer garment worn over all the others to symbolize charity and the yoke of unselfish service for God. The inner garments were pure white, while the outer ones were in what was called ecclesiastical colors, which spoke a language of their own; a language of faith and love, as does the entire liturgical Mass. Today's colors were violet: the color of humility and penance. All of these vestments were originally ordinary garments of the ancient Roman world, the priest wearing them as a witness to the historical continuity of the Catholic Church.

At 7:28 am, Father Zak pushed the button in the sacristy that controlled the bells hanging in the bell tower high above St. Stephen's. At exactly 7:30, the altar boys led him out onto the altar to begin the ancient Tridentine Mass. It was mostly in Latin, except for the reading of the gospel, read to the people in the vernacular, which for now in America was still English.

Everyone in the church made the sign of the cross as Father said, "IN NOMINE Patris, et Filii, et Spiritus Sancti. Amen."

"Introibo ad altare Dei," said Father Zak.

The altar boys responded, "Ad Deum qui laetificat juventutem meam."

They were praying: I come to the altar of God. The God Who gives joy to my youth.

And so the Mass had begun.

As Father Zak had left the sacristy to begin the mass, before he turned his back to the people to face the altar, he caught a glimpse of Joan Walker standing in a pew about halfway back, adjacent to the St. Philomena kneeler. She was holding one of the missals or prayer books provided for the congregation, allowing them to pray silently the English translation of the Latin prayers being quietly prayed at the altar by the priest. At some point before the Gospel was read, Joan had involuntarily begun to scan the church, taking in the exquisite beauty of the magnificent stained glass windows and the intricate detailed architecture of St. Stephen's. As she did so, she noticed a man across the aisle and just ahead of her. He was tall and lean with a sharp angled face, dark brown eyes clearly visible even from this distance. His hair was a sandy blonde color, loosely curled and only slightly combed.

"Gloria in excelsis Deo. Et in terra pax hominibus bonae voluntatis." (Glory to God in the highest. And on earth peace to men of good will.)

Joan concentrated on the prayers of mass, making every effort to follow Father Zak through the Sacred Liturgy. After all, this was the first Mass she had attended in many years. But time after time she was drawn almost mystically and against her will to the figure of the man she had noticed across the aisle. He stood erect, but with a casual athleticism of a great stored energy which seemed ready to explode into action at any instant. She wasn't sure if he was a man who might fall asleep, or a leopard ready to pounce upon its prey. Maybe he was both, she thought.

"Dominus vobiscum. Et cum spiritu tuo. Initium sancti Evangelii secundum Mattheum." (The Lord be with you. And with your spirit. The beginning of the holy Gospel according to Saint Matthew.)

Joan heard Father Zak read the Gospel about the triumphant entry of Jesus into the city of Jerusalem. She realized that it was Palm Sunday, just one week before Easter. Joan's head began to spin in a joyful, almost surreal whirlwind. She could feel herself being drawn into the bosom of her spiritual home, Holy Mother Church, but at the same time she was somewhat ashamed with the way she was distracted by a perfect stranger, someone she would probably never meet. But her attention continued to be drawn involuntarily to the man with whom she could already feel a spiritual affinity; a closeness that went beyond the mundane, normal reactions one might expect in a setting such as this. Could this be her soulmate? The reason she had come here to St. Stephen's? She dispelled these careless thoughts and felt foolish for having them.

His face belonged on Mt. Rushmore, she thought, with sharp handsome features that seemed chiseled in granite. His dark eyes, however, retained a softness that spoke of finer sensibilities. Yet, there was something emanating from him that seemed unattainable, an aloofness carefully crafted as protective walls to keep the outside world at bay. This was a man that nobody could ever really have. He would always keep a part of himself to himself. Joan decided that, if she was any judge at all, this would be an intriguing challenge for some woman, someday. Instinctively she had noticed there was no wedding ring on his left hand. And the fact that he was here attending early morning mass spoke volumes about his character.

"Suscipe, sancte Pater, omnipotens aeterne Deus, hanc immaculatam hostiam." (Accept, O Holy Father, Almighty and Eternal God, this spotless host.)

The church lights created violet flecks of sparkle coming off Father Zak's vestments as he raised the rounded, golden Patten with the unconsecrated host as an offering to God. This was but a prelude to the great act of consecration which was yet to come. It was at this point that Joan realized that she had focused most of her attention to this point of the mass on the tall man across the aisle. Someone she had never met and knew nothing about. A flush of redness ran through her body, spilling up into her face. It wasn't just embarrassment, but also jolts of buzzing excitement that ran through her body and mind. She had had some excitement in her past relationships, as few as they were, but nothing that compared to this. This made her even more embarrassed, making her even more excited, and so on, till she thought she might just explode right there in the church.

"Sanctus, Sanctus, Sanctus, Dominus Deus Sabaoth." (Holy, Holy, Holy, Lord God of Hosts.)

The altar boys had rung the bell three times announcing the beginning of a section of the mass called the Canon. The bells snapped Joan Walker out of a reverie that had left her mind swooning from the excitement of, on the one hand, being back in church, and on the other hand, having her attention being torn by the man she could no longer ignore.

This continued through various parts of the mass until the bells once again rang three times as Father Zak said, "Hoc est enim Corpus meum." (For this is my Body.) And then, "Hic est enim Calix Sanguinis mei." (For this is the Chalice of my Blood.) This was the act of consecration

Remembering When

when the bread and wine were changed into the Body and Blood of Jesus, Who was now Himself on the altar. Joan bowed her head and struck her breast three times while praying, MY LORD AND MY GOD. It was something she remembered learning at Catholic School when she was a young child.

Father Zak had reached the summit of the mass when he offered the victim to God. "-- puram hostiam, sanctam hostiam, immaculatam Panem --" (-- the pure Victim, the holy Victim, the all-perfect Victim --)

As Joan Walker joined Father Zak in offering God the Son, as a victim to God the Father, in spite of all she could do to stop herself, she was offering her heart to the tall man who was now on his knees across the aisle. When it was time to receive Our Lord in Holy Communion, Joan stayed in her pew. After not having gone to mass in many years, Joan knew she was unworthy to receive. Not until her soul had been cleansed in the Sacrament of Confession. While most of the others in church advanced up to kneel at the altar railing to receive communion, Joan noticed that the man also stayed in his place. The mass ended benignly with Father Zak and the altar boys leaving the altar in strict formation. Joan stayed in a kneeling position, noticing out of the corner of her eye, that the object of her attention stayed kneeling, too.

In the past, Joan had seen how the mind of a man can work; the coldness, the indifference, often a lack of respect and sensitivity for things that lie hidden from the five senses. Those things that really mattered, that drove us onward and then finally upward to eternal realities. But this man was definitely different. He had refrained from receiving communion which could mean that he understood the meaning of the sacrament. And when the mass ended, he continued in prayer. Father Zak and the altar boys who were attending him were busy properly folding the sacred vestments, placing them in the proper drawers. When their task was completed, Father walked out of the sacristy at precisely the moment when Joan had risen from the kneeler. She left the pew and was genuflecting before the tabernacle, which was in the center of the altar. Father was bright and vigorous this morning, smiling as he approached Joan, extending his hand in greeting.

"So you made it," he said. "Was it difficult?"

"No. I'm used to early mornings. And besides that, I was excited with the prospect of attending mass for the first time in... well, let's just say it's been a while."

As she spoke she could feel herself tingle with anticipation. It was a hunger that screamed for satisfaction. But where did this yearning originate and what was its object. These were the questions that demanded answers; answers that Joan did not possess. As they continued to speak quietly, in hushed tones, which was proper in church, Joan could feel a presence behind her. With all her might and with the speed of light, she prayed that it was him. Slowly, she turned and gazed into his face, which was even more handsome up close. His dark brown eyes immediately held her captive. Father Zak was the first to speak. Looking up slightly and behind Joan he quietly said, "Good morning, Matt." Extending his arms to lightly enfold both his guests he continued. "Joan, I'd like you to meet a new friend of mine from Arizona. Phoenix, I believe. This is Matt Brent."

Matt Brent did not exactly tower over the other two. Father Zak, himself, was several inches over 6 feet tall and Joan Walker was athletic and tall for a woman. But his slight height advantage was only the beginning. He carried with him a commanding presence that seemed to envelope everything around him. He extended his hand to Joan, and when she was slow to respond, reached down slightly and took her hand within his own.

"Good morning," he said.

Joan decided that his face was definitely Mt. Rushmore material. His dark brown eyes were mostly the size of cup saucers with an intensity that was disarming. She was reluctant to speak under the spell which he cast; her deepest secrets revealed, her darkest moments brought to light, her most basic motives completely exposed. These were her thoughts and feelings as she held his hand in a gentle handshake, concentrating intently on not gurgling, giggling or shaking about in wild frenzy.

Father Zak continued to whisper in conversation as he ushered his two companions up the center aisle to the vestibule, then through the heavy front doors to a concrete platform that spilled out into a mountain of steps, leading to the sidewalk in front of the church. Father picked up the volume in his voice as they left the church and now spoke in a normal tone.

"Duty calls, so I only have a moment. See that beautiful brick sidewalk that winds beyond the rectory? It leads it to a enchanting garden and retreat area. It's wonderfully maintained and groomed by professional landscapers who volunteer their time to St. Stephen's. It's a place where people find answers. You're both welcome to it any time you please. Gotta run now. Hope to see you both at mass tomorrow morning." And with that, Father Zak turned on his heel and was gone.

In the next instant, Matt Brent turned his face away from Joan Walker and in a brusque, harsh tone he said, "I must go as well. Goodbye." And just like that, he practically stormed off the grounds of St. Stephen's, leaving Joan bewildered and alone.

Although she was crushed by her encounter with Matt Brent outside the church, Joan maintained her poise and came away with a certain inner peace she hadn't had since her childhood. The embarrassment she harbored from the intense attraction she felt for him had almost completely disappeared as well. This she counted as a singular grace from God. And after all, despite her bad luck with men in the past, she was still a red-blooded American girl and so there it is. But when she returned to St. Stephen's for Monday morning mass, her first tendency was to look for Matt Brent. He wasn't there, so she shrugged her shoulders to no one in particular, and settled down in the pew.

That afternoon Joan visited the garden behind the rectory. It was quiet, and she was alone. It was early season so the garden beds and medium sized trees were only beginning to show the spark of life. But you could tell that the gardeners had already been busy, as everything was neat, clean, raked and landscaped. All was ready for the first growth of spring. Over the next hour Joan walked, prayed and thought. About faith, about life, about love. Things began to sort out in her mind and spirit, making more sense. Even the scars she carried on her heart took on a nameless meaning. She was the right girl, in the right place, at the right time. And there in the silence of the garden, with only the chirping of a spring sparrow, she knew that things were starting to move very quickly. 'Hang on Joanie,' she thought. 'You're in for the ride of your life.'

It was Holy Week, the week before Easter, and Joan

had no thought of leaving town or St. Stephen's. Tuesday morning mass was especially significant, leaving her with an inner glow that was palpable. That afternoon, in the garden, the air was light with muted rays of sun pouring out over the trees and flower beds. Joan was praying: 'St. Philomena, Powerful with God, pray for us. St. Philomena, Powerful with God, pray for us.' Over and over. As Joan walked the brick paths, she could feel a presence she remembered after mass on Sunday. There was power in it. Was she afraid? Or excited? Or both?! The wooden gate to the garden slowly opened, and there standing before her was the tall, chiseled figure of Matt Brent.

"I'm disturbing your solitude," he said.

"Not at all. I was just thinking that I could use some company."

He passed through the doorway and walked the path till he was near Joan, but without invading her personal space. It was close enough for Joan.

"Look, about Sunday --"

"Shhhhh --" she said, putting her finger up to her lips. "Believe me, I understand. Shall we sit down." She gestured to a sturdy wooden bench.

"No, let's walk."

"So, you're from Arizona."

"Yes. Phoenix is my hometown.

"What brings you to Upstate New York?"

"Business. I'm in import/export. Grains, produce, commodities."

They chatted for several minutes; about what was a mystery to Joan. All she would later remember was the way their eyes locked together in a tight grip.

"I've been going to mass in the morning. I haven't seen you there," she said.

"Will you be there tomorrow morning?" he said.

"Yes."

Matt turned from Joan and walked the path back to the wooden gate. Before passing through he turned to her and said, "So will I."

The following morning, they sat together at mass with appropriate spacing between them. Actually they were just a little closer than that. After mass, Father Zak came out to greet them. After exchanging pleasantries, Father said, "I've noticed that we aren't receiving Holy Communion yet."

"Yes, Father. When are confessions scheduled?" Joan said. Her face was warming with surprise at the way she blurted that out.

"Why not right now," Father Zak said, gesturing to one of the confessionals at the back of the church.

Joan and Matt gazed at each other momentarily. Things were really moving fast.

"No time like the present," Matt said.

"You go first," she said.

"Alright. Did you bring a book?"

"Never mind. I'm fine."

After confession, they left the church together and parted outside. They spent the rest of Holy Week together, attending mass and services, including praying silently for three hours from noon till three o'clock on Good Friday. This was the time that Jesus hung dying on the cross. Many hours were also spent together in the retreat garden. They walked and sat and talked; both of them at ease with each other, willing to open themselves up to the other. It was during this time that a closeness grew from their shared experiences. Their troubled youth, wayward adolescence and broken adulthood. Matt was thirty-six years old; nine years older than Joan. She liked that. Both had been betrayed in their relationships and considered it impossible to ever find the right one, the only one. That is, up until now. When Easter Sunday finally arrived they were both bright and vibrant with anticipation. Christ had risen from the dead and the world seemed filled to the brim with life. After receiving Holy Communion, they knelt in gratitude for the grace of God which brought them back to the faith of their fathers. Father Zak's sermon had centered around second chances given to those with the courage to take them. This was a message that Matt Brent and Joan Walker took to heart. When mass was over they continued kneeling in prayer, until finally Father Zach came out of the sacristy.

"You both came to St. Stephen's looking for answers. Have you found any?" he asked.

A grin curled around the lips of Joan Walker. "I think you know the answer to that, Father," she said.

Father Casey Zak stood at the altar railing and watched them leave St. Stephen's together. Matt closed the doors of the church and offered his hand to Joan. "Are you ready for this?" he said.

"You bet I am. Let's go."

As they walked, holding hands, down the multitude of steps to the sidewalk, Matt said, "Little did I know what was waiting for me here at St. Stephen's when I left Johnson City."

"Johnson City? I thought you said you were from Phoenix, Arizona."

"Yes, originally. But I had moved to Johnson City a year ago for business reasons."

"Me, too. I mean, I came here from Johnson City, too. What brought you to St. Stephen's, Matt?"

"I found them in a brochure."

"No. I mean, why did you come here?"

"Well, it's kind of embarrassing really."

"Please tell me."

"Okay. Some friends of mine felt that after all I had been through they would do me a favor, and without my knowing it they set me up with... well, if you must know... I was running away from a blind date."

About the Authors

Jeffrey A. Angus lives in Auburn with his wife Bonny. He likes writing, golf, football, and food. (And not always in that order.) Jeffrey enjoys the work he does with Norgus Press and is very excited to offer the opportunity for new writers to publish their work for others to enjoy. You can find more of his poetry in *A Collage of Words* and *Watercolor Words*, also published by Norgus Press.

Rick Ducayne has his own barber shop in Auburn N.Y. He is married to his wonderful wife Judy and has nine children, each special in their own way. He is involved in the community and his church, and if you ever want to know anything about Auburn, classic radio or T.V. sit in his shop and he would be glad to talk about it with you. His friendly smile welcomes you whenever you see him.

Gabrielle R. West lives in Elbridge, NY with her parents Teena and Marty Williams. She will be entering into her sophomore year at Jordan Elbridge High School in September 2014. Gabrielle loves to express herself in her poetry and drawings. She is a proud member of the Jordan Elbridge Marching

Eagles and is involved in numerous clubs in school, including Art Club. She is an avid artist and storywriter. She would like to thank Jeff Angus and Norgus Press for letting her express her thoughts on something more than a scratch pad.